T0065411

MANLY PARTS

J.S.CHRISTIAN

authorHOUSE®

AuthorHouse™
1663 Liberty Drive
Bloomington, IN 47403
www.authorhouse.com
Phone: 833-262-8899

Published by AuthorHouse 02/10/2021

ISBN: 978-1-6655-1347-0 (sc)
ISBN: 978-1-6655-1346-3 (e)

POETRY ODE

In this ode to you from poetry
I'm drunk without a drink

Verbose with still an audience
Allowed to overthink

Deep with both deep and shallow
Ends.
Touching without fingerprints

Though injected and reflected;
Complicated common sense.

Clean immersion in the trenches
High atop with ocean views

And all this just
To get inside of you.

I'M GAME

I promise you I am trying to try

I have no ready alibi

Just hot popcorn, cold beer,

Remote close by

I'm not thinking.

Not feeling a thing.

Blah blah something about a ring

I only heard a part of

What you were saying

Your friends; they all...

Your parents called...

My mind and eyes are on the ball

Right now Falcons and Patriots are playing

Must cut you off

I'm being soft

Heat is melting my mug frost

Your daily crisis gets time out.
Delay.

While I am watching

football games today

DOGS

When dogs go walk their people
It's hard not to smile

Small or large, the dog's in charge
Watch your step now.
There's a pile...

Of people trained to do cool tricks.
You should see what I saw

Without a word canine commands
Meal service hand to paw

And belly rubs
warm bubbled tubs.
They take their time but come

When called to get a treat for it.
Who says that dogs are dumb?

MAKING LOVE

The ingredients are simple
The process very hard

The details of the recipe
Will not fit on one card

So many spoons and pinches
At times it won't make sense

At times you'll think all ready
Discover missed Ingredients

Stirring up is easy though
can make a mess

Done right in correct measures
Taste buds will be blessed

Preheat to right temperature and
Patiently await

Product proof of good processing
In the Love we make

SKIPPING ROBE

One two
Unbuckle my shoes
Three four
Close the door
Five six
(Yes, sleeping kids!)

Now 7,

Seven, Seven...

8, 9, 10

Again!

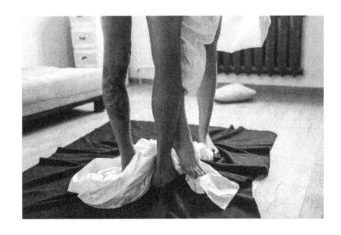

SCORED

Traffic backed up right behind me

Noisy neighbors moved away

So I can finally watch my games in peace

starting today

The grocery store restocked libations

My favorite cheap brand was

on clearance

My rooftop talker has to work late so

no game time interference

My outlaw in-laws visit plans changed.

Thank you Lord.

Then with just moments left to play,

my winning team has also

SCORED!

FULL FILL

we're topped off
no more vacancies

all sold out
no standing room

not even making
waiting list

posting no sign

"returning soon"

the border's closed
the wall is built

it's up
it's very high

taking no more
applications

any pending
get denied

banning scammers,
hatred, ignorance,

racists, looters, fools

only allowing investors
in schools

EASY YES

When you discourage children

Try to make disabled flee

School bells should have warnings.

About Disparaging Decrees

When the question

Can you help me?

Posed by any children come

It shouldn't matter how the child looks

Who the question's coming from.

The answer should be easy

Y-E-S or Yes or YES!

We will do what we can

With you for you;
for whole U.S.

Not feign to teach; place funds in reach then push the child away

REEL SMART

I'm a bright guy.
I know what to do
I know how to
drown out noise

Have a clever way
for when I want
to hang out
with the boys

I keep a pack, pad
and pen handy
when grocery list
Instructions come

Know fishing
Hot spots and
How to get there
From my home

(sometimes it takes too long)

Catch and release
Real life lessons
In colors not
just white and black

They are Life Long
Should have
a theme song

And a rod and reel
in back"

REAL MEN

Real men 'hit on' women
(just **on**)
With no real contact
Save the fury for the boxing ring
The gym
The field and track

Real men encourage their kids
Follow through as biggest fans
Appreciate real women
Make requests. Never demands.

Have a soft spot for their mothers
Try to walk on Father's way
Know it's manly when men fear God
Are not ashamed to pray

For neighbors, country, world peace.
For selves; eternal life.
Our country needs more real men

Signed,
a Real man's wife

ONE DAY

One day
correct will not be political
Right
Will only be direction
Left
Will be the other way
They will join at intersections

Children will all be childish
Distinguishable
From adults
Resolution will most matter
Not shaming those at fault

Worth will not be determined
on sight, only by heart deed
Fair honest ways
Will lead the way
One day
One day
One day
I say
Can we please?

FRIENDS

My friends have feet
and fingerprints

And pulses palms and
Common sense

They know most
Of my favorite songs

Occasionally
Sing along

Real friends know
How to make you laugh

And can complete
Your paragraphs

When you ramble, ramble, ramble
Way too long

They circle back when
Things seem odd

Compared to times
When you were not

Impacted by
Virtually
Everything

They wipe your tears
You can bet
They don't mind
A shoulder wet

Or the fact you try
Though oh, so
Humbly sing"

CLICK

Not going to rhyme this
This is serious.
Debilitating
Depression
Cancel
Culture
Paper thin
Moral Fiber
Mythical middle classes

Someone turn on the lights!

LET'S TALK

I don't know how to talk to you
I do know what to say
I have unsown seeds for fertile soil
I want to spread your way

We have to make
Connections

Moving forward
We should step

In the same direction
Our country needs the help

To heal our pain,
Unite again
before we fall apart

I don't know how to talk to you
I know this is a start

CONNECTIONS

When you break connect i o n s

You

    l o s e

       P

       O

       W

       e

       R.

HIGHER CONSTRUCT

We hold these truths of having
Been created equal tightly

In so doing, we remind ourselves in prayer
daily and nightly

Focus on goodness, self rely
Self sustain, boldly cry

Be true to who and how God made you stand

Educate where lessons come
Never hold out flattened palms
To beg
Instead rotate to shake a hand

(Your brothers hand)

Only look down
To tie your shoes and to teach young
Children who

Look up to you
As good women
And men

Seek favor only from above
Love all people. Receive love.
Again.

FOLD OVER

I try to never confuse
Who I am
With
With
Who I am
They are not the same

THIS IS FUNNY

Ok, now this is funny

Just because I say it is

I don't have to get approval

For laugh lines

I don't giggle

Or gerflaffle

I do slapjacks while you waffle

I just made this up because

Those two words rhymed

So this is slip and falling funny

I like to laugh but I'm no dummy

I know to look away

So all seems fine.

Then walk away to Ha-Ha-

Have a real good time

JIM, JACK AND STOLI

You, Jim, Jack and Stoli
Should not climb back inside
that car
Put the keys down on the bar please
Since you won't get very far
Unless you're willing
to risk killing,
Cars cannot climb up in trees
And little babies strapped
in car seats
Can't bear the weight
of SUVs.
So you, Jim, Jack and Stoli
Need to vote on what to do
Take the night to sleep it off
Or go hurt a child or two.

GOOD GUY

He is not God
so why the
trembling?
He is not God
so why the
fear?

He's just a man
who has no plan to hurt you.

He's huge, that's true
Though so are you

With what it is you

Plan to do
To hurt him.

When you call to cause alarm

See your father
See your son

See our Father and His son

See a man there who has...

No plans to hurt you

WORKING OUT

Seeeeee, I've been working out
more lately
Changing up my weight routine
Cut way down caloric intake

Carbs in my diet are unseen

Chances are won't recognize me

Chiseled progress minus beer

Count still that I am nothing like...

(chest of chiseled pictured here)

NO BLACKS ALOUD

"Why'd you have to come
change things?!"
Mary Eller asked

"We were all Right.
We were all White.
Now you are here.
You're Black."

He gave it thought
paused as he
ought.
Using initials
of her name

Said,
Hey ME, you chose
to color this,

My view and yours
are same.

SOCIAL CONSTRUCT

It's not that we don't want you here
We just don't want to see you

Or talk to you
Or walk with you
And certainly not free you

From the burden of oppression
Or the onset of depression

That ensues
Ostracizing is much easier
We've worked too hard to be here

To not work hard
To not see you here too.

REUNION DANCE

When won't look at them
but stare at everything they do
and report it as suspicious
because hue

Instead look and see
as future friends for you.

No need rehearse greets in your mind
A heart sincere will reflect kind
Any missteps are forgiven
in advance.

So, yeah; just walk this way
Let your words say
what they'll say
We'll do fine in Unifying
Awkward dance.

HAPPY DAYS

I'm giving me Authority
to be Happy.

To have some days when I don't have to pack guilt in my lunch

I'll carry a backpack stuffed with apologies for folks

I unintentionally offend a bunch

I will lead with "Hello, I'm Sorry.
Who...
What in the hell are you?"

I'll ignore the bumper stickers answering that question too.

I won't ponder. I will...

Be Happy. Be Honest. Be Me.

It's my Happy Day. On Happy Days, I'm free.

I don't have to read it, get it, apologize for it, or DARE

It's in the bag. I'm Happy.

I don't CARE.

NEWS FLASH!

There are some Whites who are not millionaires.

In fact, there are many on public welfare.

Who are not racists, lying hatefuls chasing others out of town.

Who could care less whose car is best or that your skin is brown.

We have bills, also get chills when flashing lights go by

And pray today is not the day another young Black man will die

BROTHERS

One steps forward.
Two step back.
Archaic movements.
Whites and Blacks.
Symbiotic seems terrific.
Less divided. Less horrific
than the truth we aren't the same.
Yet we are...with same last names.

INSIDER

When you live inside

Whale's belly,
You see
Wha
Whe

Who
He eats

Just prior to digested self
once a delicious treat

STEREOS

Not all of them are like that
I've met a few who don't.

Some I've seen will do those things
Though some certainly won't.

When you say "they" name two
or more for evidence or else,

You exaggerate and overstate.
Just wasting precious breath.

Base any 'they' on hearsay and you are surely wrong
Or just prejudice and need to change
yourself, your views, that song

JUSTICE SCOUT RECRUIT

I believe in playing ball so, on the cause, I'm sold.

However, if you want me on your team this must unfold:

1. Approach me real and proper. Make your message clear.
2. Don't shout. This turns me off. There's a chance that I won't hear.
3. Do your homework. Know yourself. Know exactly who I am.
4. Don't hit me with a bat. This hurts us both; it kills the plan.
5. Have and share your vision of my role on your team.
6. Use sincere semantics clearly stating what you mean.

That's it. Just this. Commit.

Phone in and I will take your call.

The country says move quickly.

Let's play ball!

DISMOUNT

Can you get off my back
A minute?

Give me one day without
You in it?

And me starring in your nagging
Hall of Shame

I do my best so cease the stress

It's the weight I carry here that's most
to blame.

I can't make light of anything

you even criticized the ring

the house. the car.
when near.
afar.
the everything.

so I ask just for a minute

get off my back

so we can win this

Carry love for life.

For Christsake

In His name.

WHYT

I'm White

I am not the boogie man

I don't feel privileged

Understand

My understanding's

From my point of view

It's tough to feel

When never touched

I'll try to do this better

MUCH

I may need Empathy

From You

And you

You too.

YOU TOO

I apologize for whatever was done to
by whomever did whatever was done to you

I promise it wasn't me or,
to my knowledge, any man

I know...or think I know or ever knew...

Just
Know
That Man
Wasn't Me

Nor will it ever be.

Likewise, try not to ever be, a YOU TOO

That person who will do
the something to...

COMPATIBLE

We can agree on many things
Though I'm fries, you onion rings.
We both prefer our coffee without cream
I'm a vegan
You eat meat
Neither like the middle seat.
When we don't know the words to songs, we fake them.
I like water, you snow ski
I am Jewish
You, Hindi
As sports go, we both can leave or take them
I'm a seltzer, you drink bolt
Neither laugh at racist jokes
Or make them

COLOR BLIND

When you claim to see no color

It makes me scratch my head.

Driving must be hard for you

No green, yellow, or red.

TRASH TALKING

Amounts of land aren't infinite.
Amounts of trash certainly are
It's not acknowledged as a crisis
At least not so far

We need somewhere to put all of our dry bones and
All the trash we all like to produce
Or plan to live on scented hills,
Plan to mass olfactory kill.
And never ever plan
To reproduce

DANCERS

Want to see something funny?
Watch me dance. Oh my.
I enjoy the music. Moving.
Mentally. I try.

If square dancing's what we're doing
then I'm trying to dosey doe
If we're waltzing then I'm boxing
probably stepping on your toes

I can two-step with enough prep
make it look good in the dark
Or just chair dance in my khaki pants
Wave my arms and bark.

Sure, laugh when you see moves and music
mostly out of sync.
Too left/right leaners dance bad as we think!

HEARTY FARMER

Greg was a hearty farmer with lots of land to care.
Uncomplicated. Unencumbered.
Just wheat and steer out there.

Farm traffic had no stoplights
Tractor drivers never yelled.
He sped 10 miles per hour
rolling
rolling
up hay bales.

To communicate with cattle he didn't have to text
There were never social battles.
He really could care less.

His hearty seeds made feed
some vegetables,
for food
and then

He'd grab a hearty handful.

Start the process o'er again.

And again.
And again.

ALGORITHM CRUSH

It's apparent she has a crush on me

She knows everything I do

She follows me so she can see

just where I am and with who

I wish she would get a life
(or a husband or a wife)
So that I could just go on with mine.

I've had enough.
I will go hit her
"power off!"
Whew!
Now I am fine.

SSSH

Recall when you
Were very small
A tiny tike
So young

You'd say too much
Incite firm touch
And order
"bite your tongue!"

You're older now
Wiser somehow
Grown discernment
when to stop

Refrain from rage
Never engage
Armed angry
Packing cops

Silence resembles
Solace
Strong ground
Standing ridicule

Have thoughts more
Clear focused then
Drown out angry fools.

Nagging words for
Sayings sake
Sound as
Seething water drops

Beckons wrenches for repairing
sends husbands to the roof tops

So sssh...yes, sssh
And listen
For His cue to share your song

Trust you'll have a symphony

And full use of your tongue.

MAGIC SPRAY

White friends don't like
my friends are Black
Black that my friends
are White
My Lefts can't stand
that I make plans with ones
who are on Right

My hipsters snub my nerdy,
my Foodies snub my Cruisers
My kingdom
for a magic spray
for prejudice diffusers.

ALL HIS

All that I know God taught me

All that I own God bought me

All that I have God gave me

All that I am God made me.

LIFE IS LIKE

Filled with too much hot air
Bound to float away
Held too tightly
Bound to burst
then nothing left to play
with
Knowing just how little can
control before deploys

Just sit back, go kick back

AND ENJOY!

BREAKTHROUGH

I did Catholicism easily
it taught me how to Guilt

And patience was a piece of cake
it's how Rome was built

Great Wall of China - easy climb was just a little hill

Decathlons. Yeah bring em on!
Just 10 sports slots to fill

but success?
oh, what a mess!
a challenge
just a dream

I can't seem to master that
Don't know what it means

My more needs more
and bigger better building
One last try.

Lord:
"show me your Love is the more".
Success!
Now satisfied.

IT'S OKAY

Sometimes it's OK

To not be OK

Acceptable not to be fine.

To need just a minute

To not be with it.

To want just

a little more time...

To be OK.

HELP

Here's how can engage our impacted

Ostracized

Now outcast

And impaired...

Not write them off
but care enough
to see them as people.
If DARE.

(go help get them

some help

somewhere)

Ask name
share the same
Then sit. Listen.

Silent pause
may just cause
a blank stare

Time to offer a soothing
outreach and affirm
you are sincerely
Present and you
CARE

QUINT-TREE-CENTRAL ©

The 5th tree behind
the other four
took just as long to grow
it's just as tall
it's just as thick
Yet other arbors steal the show
The first tree is most visible.
The second gets the breeze.
Tree three can feel
sun glimmers still.
The fourth is within reach.

The fifth is nature's humble fort
stands strong and
layers in rings.
Holds blue jays in the wind, sways, as the robins perch
to sing.
the fifth's the quintessential
of asking for nothing more
than to be
the only tree
obscured yet clandestine adored.

DICTION

Practice using real words.
Taste them before you say them.

If lyrics are sour or profane,
don't bother to play them.

Ponder what words' purpose is.
If there is none, be quiet.

Inciting ones just kill the fun
and that's how we start riots.

LOOK AT ME

I sat next to you

on the train today.
You weren't quite sure
just what to say.
To me sitting here
chatting with myself.
Did you not here
my cry for help?
I looked around to
see if you
could here the noises,
popping too.
I'm guessing no.
You moved away.
You weren't quite sure
just what to say.

NO ONE

I've never known someone of None.
Created from themselves
Conceived from own seed planted, rooted
grown from No One else.
Yet here we are
Adrift
Afar
Aloft
Alone
Astray

No one's Some of

Someone's son

Detached then blown away.

FURNITURE

Coffee table on all four legs just
upped and walked away.
The sofa slowly followed suit.
You had beans today.

The television looks at you
It's very turned off. Sighs.
You too often change the channel
Based on who you're sitting by.
They're leaving.
You can stand and Tweet.
Entertain yourself by text
Keep treating them like objects,
People next

AH C'MON!

If you have lived
A lots of years
And none of them
Are hazy

You're either
A big liar or
Going crazy

If you have never wanted more
than you had
Tried to ignore
That people in your life can
forsake you

Always happy no matter
where life takes you.

Then I'll try not to wake you.

FISHING TRIP

Stocked lake
Tackle box
Bobber Hooks
Luuuures

Bait
Ties
Cheap beer

Big one!
Suuure...
Catch and Release
Waiting in waders

Ones that got away
Rod
Boat
Reel in
Real fish you caught today.

ARCHIBALD

Everyone seems
Normal within
Their scope of view

Only our outsiders

Find abnormal
What we do

When we scope back
To mirror
All in abutting lens

Then all the little children
See
What crazy really is

NO BIG DEAL

I'm Asian and my wife is Black.

It's really no big deal
Race plays no part
How either of us feel

I saw her. She was very cute. Also very smart
Her gorgeous smile drew me in, quickly melted my heart
The best thing about her
There are many I can see
Is that she also chose to fall
in love with me

PERSON EYES

Dare look a person
in their eyes
and see
their
person
otherwise
Dare see there person

Otherwise

There

NIMBY

You can't see us in the attics
Basements are too dark and dank.
We can't remember how we got here
Though are sure who should be thanked

All the

N.ot-
I.n-
M.y-
B.ack-
Y.arders

Wanting us to disappear
We have a right
to have a life and
Live anywhere
but here.

NO ONE KNOCKED

It may take a minute
Or 500 years
to recover.
This was our land
Not yours to
"Discover"

HEIRBORNE

I'm not jumping without a parachute
Or power rockets on my boots
No matter how effing sad I am

Borne. I already aced the test
My beating heart, my breath - SUCCESS!
Even when nobody gives a dayum

Though...

If I forget, can't handle it and
try to quit by winging it
Or make a choice to go out on a limb

Or, out of cash, I dash to splash.
I pray I can remember that

I'm Heir borne.

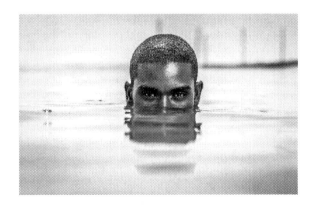

Thank God that I can swim

NOT GUILTY

I wasn't even born then
My parents owned no one
I invited most of my classmates
to my parties; out for fun.

I mean, so not everyone could
Come inside my house to play

I could meet them at the local park
And whenever they...

Would invite me over their house
I had something else to do

It was not because of race.
Well, mostly true.

FISHY

I am so American
I named my pet fish

Red

White

Blue

My little swimming patriots,
so patriotic too
We all know most pet fish don't
last for very long
I wax poetic their deaths in fishy
patriot burial songs

Red floats hardiness and valor swam from right to left
So strong so brave so upside down so newly now bereft

White purity and innocence;
he bobbled well then died
Blue was just and vigilant;

he swam from left to right

All come together in the end
fin to fin and glub glub glub

Farewell my brave patriot fish.
you swam so well.
Now Flush!

JUST BEING US

I love this country and its humanoids
It's beauty and the grace
Every perfect imperfection
Every single U.S. face

Sure I've been to Paris
Great Wall has my DNA
America is still the best
Don't care what people say

OK, we have some traffic but the Light moves us along
As we listen to the tunes too loudly blasting U.S. songs

Sure Athens, Greece is breathtaking.
Our Athens, Georgia has bulldogs!

Sure Germany has fast fancy cars.
Our U. S. rumbles Hogs!

You can have fries Nova Scotia
Or << pomme frites>> it in Quebec

Nothing beats my brother's beans and barbecue on his rear deck

We're called brash, loud and obnoxious braggards raising
too much fuss

We're just the best at being better
God bless us all
just being US!

LUCKY US

I take off my shoes on muddy days.
Nod. Fake listen what you say
Take out the trash
And try to make less of it

I put dirty laundry in one pile
Tell crude jokes
to make you smile
I know you don't like them
so I love it

I put the seat down
Kept your spirits up
When I broke your
favorite coffee cup

That I used for my
driving range indoors
I even once picked up some
bread and milk from store

You should be grateful
Who could ask for any more?

KISSING LESSON

Who in the heck came up with this?
Pressing a face to make a kiss.
The nose knows not
what to do
If running somewhere
just prior to
The coordination
about to begin
How does it start?
When does it end?
Lean in with forehead?
Lead with the chin?
A tilt to side to thwart collide
a nostril and a cheek
Eyes open wide slow pucker glide to land on lips oblique

STONE COLD

Thank you for sharing all of your warm desires and your dreams
So I can cold more easily align them with my schemes
I always take the time to memorize yours line by line
Have you empty out your quiver then tell you everything is fine
I besmirch your innocence then wink, and smile and blow kisses
slither words over polished teeth forked tongue and slimey hisses
rattler tucked beneath
all muffled Hidden
held silent and tight

then stoned faced
Try to lie with you tonight

WE'RE GONNA

If you came
for a fight
We're gonna
Let me show you
my guns

If you came
For a bite
I'm gonna
Get my jacket on

If you came to steal
My heart
Not gonna
It's under lock and key

If you came for love
We're gonna
Have to wait and see

If you're gonna wanna
Fall in love with me

HIDE N' SEEK

When you close your eyes we still see you.
Prolonged
Doing so
You can see
Us in
Nightmares
And Dreams.
The best thing it seems
Is to wake up and stay woke.
Knowing...

We're not going away.
Here we are
Here we'll stay
This is no time to play Hide and Seek

FIRST PLAQUES

I'm Hispanic
I don't understand why we still denote 1st Blacks
I know it's meant to celebrate.
I just need some more facts

Are we proud of their accomplishments
Or the fact they were held back?
for so many years so firsts are really 'See Suppression' plaques?

I was born here. It gets questioned.
Sanchez is my family name.
But 1st Blacks are Smiths and Washingtons
We all know where they came...

from what I've seen, the 1st Blacks descend direct your seed

So "1st Blacks of Our Family" is how the plaques should read

NEW NEW SOUTH

Grady of The New South cries out

"now it is your turn!"

This place is trying to slip apart
go show them what you learned

That left and right and
north and south
are far more than directions

And we can't run a whole country
divided into sections

By now we should face forward
not backwards have to look

for resolution lessons
chronicled in history books.

The U.S. is us and us U.S. in the U.S.A.
Fifty parts together have to operate that way

And colors? Do they matter?
You best believe they do.

Our banners fly in bright
Red, White and Blue

PIPELINE

Schools knead placeholder dough to color and to play.

Feign to teach; place funds in reach then push the child away

Stop!

Make it right to do right
Educate
ALL KIDS AS SAME

Way cross in Waycross, Georgia
Over in Overton, Maine

Keys given 'kids' to sort, divide
Never fair as planned

Brown b. Prison Pipeline
Easy lessons.
Understand?

LOVE 4 COUNTRY CONFERENCE

4 years can seem like 44 marching around in wait
all are related although belated it's never too late
4 this resolution conference for us to finally see the

L.ove
O.rder
R.econciliation (moral)
D.iplomacy

Love of God and self and others
Order and a calm resolve
Reconciliation mindset
Diplomacy: true Moral one

Start at home to show alliance
World reliance happens next
Show our family blood is thicker
Share our **Unity** progress

Unity must be intention if intend walk through the door
Progressed Success past point of venting merely; nothing more

It's time 4 talking
Time 4 listening
Time 4 resolving
Time 4 real care

Weapons held but down.
unloaded.
what happens here is everywhere
and everyone. All men.
What's shot out here hits everywhere.

LIKE IS LIKE

Different is easier
Much easier by far

Try saming love
While shaming love

Or faking love
While making love

Only being certain love
Will keep all doors ajar.

LEFT, RIGHT, LEFT

I'm out now which way to turn?

Left

Out instructions on how to earn. Now...

Right

From uniforms to clothes and shoes. Then...

Left

A bunch of memories, cammies and blues. Soo...

Right

After I got out I came to find, I've...

Left

a bunch and best ...me behind.

Right

Now figuring out what's

Left and right to do

When it's not...

Right.What's.**Left**.of.**You**.

EXIT STAGE LIFE

The instructions were to be
this way
To eat this way then that
To come this time to
turn back, line up
Never dare get fat

To wear those shoes polish those boots
Still black but make them shine
To march this way and always say that everything is fine

To use our pens
Get issued friends and paper and green socks

You're leaving now so realize the door behind you locks

Keep memories. PTSD. Your children, your ex-wife

No outdoctrination here.
Go. Exit now stage life.

BATTLE FATIGUES

The good news is
all are synced
Hard corps ready
in a blink
Battle fatigues
Ready for a fight

But why at home?
We are all one
On the same team
Already done

and too fatigued
to battle now.
No battles now. Gnight.

HEY OFFICERS

Calling on fellow officers.
Calling on all my men.

(In gender general warrior sense; no intent to offend)

We've a Higher mission calling now. A new non-battle plan.

To use some class, get off our ass and help preserve this land.

I holler from the inside. I don't know the folks out there.

Nor do they apparently.
Imports from everywhere.

Let's wear ball caps to cover; show support of our home teams

(the 50+ amongst us know exactly what I mean)

Not ostracize the allies;.
once cheered on with pride

We now sit afar in quarantine instead of alongside

When we regroup, I know we will, let's cheer for the same team

Or kiss the things we stood for bye. Pack our gear and leave.

Me? I'm going nowhere. You should stay your somewhere too.

To lead all by example to get this country through.

I KNOW, not just believe, we can help make things here better

We took an Oath and all avowed keep the U.S. held together!

HANG ON!

Hang on little brother there's

always something else to do

This is temporary. You are permanently you.

Together you and I will make it through!

So hang on little brother.
Just reach up and grab my hand.
Know that God would never give you more than you could stand.

Remember your best yesterday. Go visit in your mind.
See this as the day before.
Now wasn't that a real good time!

(Together you and I will make it through!)

Lay it down! Don't hesitate;
mind and body deep in prayer.

Yeah, it's manly crying out.
You're not the only soul in there.

Whether alone aloud
hidden in crowd.
There's always something else to do.
(Together you and I will make it through!

Yes, God will pull us through

WATERWAYS

When I drink the water
I don't analyze the elements
I'm thirsty. Water's wet.
My throat is dry.

So with two
hydrogen
Hydrations

One oxygen
Oxygenated

Parched assurance
On the water I rely

Likewise a spirit
Can get dried out
Fears and tears all
Can get cried out

Earthly elements can offer
Only grief

So choose to take it
Higher
Drink the word to
douse the fire
Cool the flames with
Holy Waters of belief.

SINGLE LOADED

Every single day I wake up
with the rising sun
Hopes and prayers are single
loaded. Up. Do not require my gun.

There are...
Investigations, Clues,
My badge, a belt, and some
blues.

Detective. Complete.
Detailed reports of what is out there happening on our streets.
For all the calls, the cars, the codes, **not a single one will say**
"Took no precautions on the case; harmed citizens today"

CHOSEN OUTFITS

The group of us decided before training even began,
That right was right, not Black or White.
Good guys should always win.
Most of us still know the difference.
For all of us, there're judgment calls.
It hurts when bad guys get away
And that the good ones sometimes fall.
We promise. Promise. Promise.
No one signed up to heed a call
other than protect and serve,
protect and serve you
One and all.

YOU ARE WELCOMED

We know if you only knew what we endure just so you
May have calm and peaceful sleep at night
There would be a lot less stress.
Civility.
No more protests.
Tangent chaos is not our oversight
We do our best
(even thankless)
to protect while standing tall
Rest assured.
We're here to serve.
Answer your calls.

50+50

Numbers are ripe
for resolution
50/50 is a tie

Something new
Not compromising
100 percent
Testify

THANK YOU

Thank you Lord

For this Day

And every thing

It brings my way

And thank you for

A voice to pray

You'll guide my thoughts

And what I say.

As I listen and obey.

"WE GET BETTER"

'I's' are solo pronoun Individuals

'Me's' are the objects
Speaking of the same

Memes are 'I' created designations

'We's' view and use to mock another's name

'They's' are the two or more I's in agreement

Who see other I's as opposite their they

Who may have hurt
Wanting to gain

Address the mess behind the pain

Longing for empathy for

mental angst they weigh

While the common space of Counselor sits empty

Room for I's Me's They's and Them's beckon all in

We will get Better

Need is Dire

We will get Smarter

We will go Higher

We will get up; come out

Time better spend.

The End.

ABOUT THE AUTHOR

J. S. Christian taught English Literature to mostly engineering majors at the U.S. Naval Academy. The former military officer and Pepperdine University School of Law alum now lives on the U. S. west coast. This book is dedicated to all past, present and future fans of poetry.

"You are Welcomed".

Printed in the United States
by Baker & Taylor Publisher Services